80 DELICIOUS
LOW CARB SMOOTHIES
FOR WEIGHT LOSS, ENERGY, AND OPTIMAL HEALTH

Copyright 2015 © Linda Stevens

All Rights Reserved.

Disclaimer

All rights Reserved. No part of this publication or the information in it may be quoted from or reproduced in any form by means such as printing, scanning, photocopying or otherwise without prior written permission of the copyright holder.

Disclaimer and Terms of Use: Effort has been made to ensure that the information in this book is accurate and complete, however, the author and the publisher do not warrant the accuracy of the information, text and graphics contained within the book due to the rapidly changing nature of science, research, known and unknown facts and internet. The Author and the publisher do not hold any responsibility for errors, omissions or contrary interpretation of the subject matter herein. This book is presented solely for motivational and informational purposes only.

Introduction

Congratulations on making the decision to embark on a journey to a healthy lifestyle! There are many benefits to a low carb diet including: weight loss – even when not consciously restricting calories, reduced blood glucose for diabetics and pre-diabetics, increased HDL ("good" cholesterol), and decreased blood pressure. Some other great advantages of a low carb diet as reported in many research studies include increased energy, reduced sugar cravings, improved triglycerides and lower blood insulin level.

If you have chosen to eat a low carb diet, you may be looking for delicious snack and smoothie recipes that add variety to your menu. This low carb smoothie cookbook will provide you with some of the very best mouth-watering smoothie recipes for breakfast or any time you're in the mood for a delicious low carb snack. Minty Blast, Emerald Detoxifier, or Avocado Coconut Smoothie are just some of the tasty recipes that you will find in this cookbook.

Low carb smoothies are a great way to increase your nutrient intake without breaking any carnal rules. Each smoothie in this book contains less than 15 grams net carbohydrates per serving! They are infinitely a lot healthier than buying smoothies at your local smoothie places, stores or even online. Most of these smoothies also contain some type of healthy fat, which in itself is a great addition to a typical day on the low carb diet. Introducing low carb smoothies to your routine is one of the best and versatile ways to improve your health. Not only are they quick and easy to make but they also contain vast amounts of vitamins, minerals, phytonutrients and fiber. It can be quite difficult to get all your servings of fruits and vegetables on a daily basis. Smoothies provide us with an optimal way to consume the recommended number of servings of fruits and vegetables and load up on antioxidants and other cancer fighting agents at the same time.

Smoothies are not a universally healthy option. Simply blending your breakfast doesn't ensure you've made a healthy choice! Smoothies high in processed sugars and fats can be just as bad as processed bread and sweetened breakfast cereals. Many common smoothie recipes fall into this trap by including fruit juices, sweetened yogurts and processed honeys. This book describes low carb smoothies for the active and health conscious individual. They are delicious, satisfying and will provide you with energy all day long. They are also rich in various superfoods such as kale, spinach, berries, nuts and seeds. You will be amazed how different you will feel after just one week of implementing these healthy treats into your daily routine.

Table Of Contents

Superfood Low Carb Smoothies 19

Grape Basil Smoothie 20

Cherry Cinnmon Smoothie 23

Minty Blast Smoothie 25

Blackberry Chia Smoothie 27

Emerald Detoxifier 30

Superfood Salad Smoothie 33

Fat Fighters and Metabolism Boosters 35

Ginger and Pineapple Smoothie 36

Apple and Pecan Smoothie 38

Strawberry Blueberry Smoothie 40

Apple Cinnamon Smoothie 42

Matcha and Almond Smoothie 44

Matcha and Avocado Smoothie 46

Pineapple Blueberry Smoothie 48

Strawberry Mint Smoothie 50

Metabolism Booster Smoothie 52

Pomegranate Smoothie 54

Instant Fat Fighter Smoothie 56

High Protein Low Carb Smoothies 59

Vanilla Heaven Smoothie 60

Almond Pineapple Smoothie 62

Chocolate Peanut Butter Smoothie 64

Avocado Almond Smoothie 66

Blueberry Spinach Smoothie 68

Almond Cinnamon Smoothie 70

Polka Dot Smoothie 72

Almond Butter Smoothie 74

High Power Smoothie 76

Chocolate and Peanut Smoothie 78

Spinach Avocado Smoothie 80

Blueberry Power Protein Smoothie 82

Pure Protein Smoothie 84

Apple Protein Smoothies 86

Energizing Smoothie Recipes 89

Sunshine Smoothie 90

Coffee Lover Smoothie 92

Berry-Licious Blast Smoothie 94

Avocado Coconut Smoothie 96

Egg and Melon Smoothie 98

Morella Cherry Smoothie 100

Raspberry Dream Smoothie 102

Kale Cherry Booster Smoothie 104

Blueberry Almond Power Smoothie 106

Berries and Spinach Smoothie 108

Berries Medley 110

Orange Smoothie 112

Coffee Flavored Smoothie 114

Tropical Berry Smoothie 116

Soy Protein smoothie 118

Non-Dairy Strawberry Smoothie 120

Banana, Mint, and Basil Smoothie 122

Mango, Banana, and Strawberry Smoothie 124

Fruit and Veggie Smoothie 126

Kiwi Goodness Smoothie 128

Breakfast Smoothie Recipes 131

Cocoa Macademia Smoothie 132

Strawberries and Cream Smoothie 134

Chocolate Raspberry Smoothie 136

Berry Mint Smoothie 138

Strawberry Raspberry Bliss Smoothie 140

Mango & Peach Surprise 142
Apple-licious Banana n' Nuts 144
Green Breakfast Smoothie 146
Berry Breakfast Low Carb Smoothie 148
Strawberry Splash Breakfast Smoothie 150
Pumpkin Spice Smoothie 152
Sweet and Creamy Chocolate Smoothie 154
Cappuccino Egg Cream Low Carb Smoothie ... 156
Strawberry Tofu Power Smoothie 158

Green Smoothie Recipes **161**
Go Green Smoothie 162
Power-up Punch 164
Green Godess 166
Spinach and Cucumber Smoothie 168
Green Salad Smoothie 170
Kale Madness Smoothie 172
Natural Energizer Smoothie 174
Green AC Booseter 176
Cool Cucumber Smoothie 178
Fresh Herbs Smoothie 180
Avocado Powerhouse 182

9

Green Detoxifier Smoothie 184
Green Pineapple Paradise 186
Tropical Blast 188
Energizing Smoothie 190
Shamrock Green Smoothie 191
Skin Cleanser Smoothie 193

Conclusion **195**

Protein

Proteins are the essential building blocks of all human cells and are particularly important in muscle tissue. Dietary protein helps the body repair damaged cells and create new ones. Protein is found in a variety of foods, though the comparative richness of meat and dairy products in proteins presents special challenges for vegans and the lactose intolerant. This book describes a variety of high-protein foods to make it easier to include dietary protein in a vegan or dairy-free diet. The high protein smoothie section utilizes protein powders, choose high quality, low carb protein powders such as Isopure Zero Carb protein powder whenever possible.

Superfoods

Superfoods are foods, which have an outsized nutritional value, a particularly rare or important nutrient, or have been shown to have a particularly beneficial effect on health. They may protect against ageing, boost immunity, assist with weight loss, or help the body's natural detoxification or healing, among many other benefits. The superfoods featured in the following list are staples of the smoothies in this guide and are listed here instead of after each individual smoothie. In addition, many of the smoothies in this guide are based around one or more superfoods.

Chia

Chia seeds are small white, brown, or black seeds from a flowering plant native to Mexico and Guatemala. The seeds have a wide variety of nutritional benefits and are essentially tasteless, making them compatible with any smoothie recipe. Chia seeds are high in fiber, manganese, calcium, and protein, and have no cholesterol.

They are also the richest plant source of omega 3 fatty acids, which improve brain health and protect against arthritis and heart disease. Omega 3 fatty acids are also great for weight loss, especially for reducing belly fat. According to recent studies, the molecules present in omega 3 fatty acids bind to special receptors on a cell and literally switch on a gene that speeds up your metabolism.

The gelatinous coating developed by chia seeds when soaked slows the rate of digestion and may reduce insulin resistance – associated with increased storage of belly fat and risk of diabetes. Chia seeds have been shown to improve blood pressure among diabetics and may reduce unhealthy triglyceride cholesterol.

To prepare chia seeds for blending, soak them in filtered water for at least 10 minutes. If refrigerated the soaked seeds will keep for up to 3 weeks. The seeds will absorb any liquid, so you could also soak them in almond milk or coconut water. Soaking gives the seeds the consistency of tapioca.

Hemp Seeds

Hemp seeds have a mild, nutty flavor comparable to pine nuts. They are an unobtrusive complement to a range of flavors, and work well in smoothies. They are extremely rich in protein, calcium, iron, zinc, magnesium, phosphorous, and antioxidants such as vitamin E. Hemp seeds also contain an omega-6 fatty acid called gamma linolenic acid or (GLA). GLA has beneficial anti-inflammatory effects, supports healthy hair and skin, and helps to improve cholesterol balance.

Coconut Water

Coconut water is a sweet, naturally occurring, liquid found inside green coconuts. It is an excellent source of electrolytes, such as potassium, essential for hydration. Coconut water also has a low glycemic index and is relatively lower in calories than comparably sweet sports drinks. Bottled coconut water is widely available, though some brands have significant quantities of added sugars.

Matcha Green Tea

Matcha is a powdered green tea made from high-quality, specially grown tealeaves. Unlike conventional green tea preparations, which only steep the leaves in hot or boiling water, Matcha provides the entire nutritional benefits available in the tealeaf. This makes Matcha a far better source of vitamins, minerals, amino acids, and antioxidants. Matcha contains a particularly potent class of antioxidants known as catechins, which counteract free radicals from UV radiation and environmental contaminants. This may prevent cell damage and may reduce the effects of ageing. Matcha also boosts the body's metabolism and contributes to weight loss.

Almond Milk

Almond milk is a high protein, low GI milk substitute made from almonds and water. It is completely lactose free and has a superior nutritional profile to other common milk substitutes such as rice milk, and soymilk.

To prepare almond milk soak 1 cup of raw almonds overnight in filtered water. Drain the almonds and place them in a blender with 3 cups of filtered water (feel free to add a vanilla bean or a few drops of vanilla essence for taste). Blend the mixture on high for 1 minute and strain through a cheesecloth. Store almond milk cold in a jar or bottle.

Almond milk is widely available in health food stores but many products are heavily sweetened. Consult the nutritional information on the packaging to select an unsweetened, low carb product.

The Single-Serve Package Method

Many of the following recipes call for less than a natural serving size of certain fruits and vegetables (e.g. half an apple). A useful strategy is to make batches of 2 or more servings of your favorite smoothie recipes in preparation for the coming week. Separate these out into Ziploc bags and store them in the freezer. Making smoothie becomes a simple matter of selecting the appropriate bag, adding the liquid base of the recipe, and blending.

Grape Basil Smoothie

When your smoothie is green in color you just know that it's going to be healthy. This particular smoothie recipe incorporates healthy ingredients such as avocado, baby spinach, grapes and ginger. Not only will this smoothie recipe help you to lose weight in the long run, but it will also help to improve your overall digestive system.

Makes: 1 Serving

Ingredients:

1 avocado, small with pits removed

2 cups of spinach, fresh and roughly torn

15 to 20 grapes, white

1 inch chunk of ginger, peeled and roughly chopped

1 handful of basil, fresh

¼ cup of sunflower seeds

½ lime, juiced

1 cup water, filtered

Directions:

Place your avocado into a freezer and allow it to freeze for at least 3 hours or until it is completely frozen. After this time remove your avocado from the freezer and scoop out the flesh from the skin.

Then using a blender, blend your avocado until it is smooth in consistency. Add in the rest of your ingredients and continue blending until the entire mixture is smooth in consistency.

Pour your freshly made smoothie mixture into tall drinking glasses and top with shaved iced. Serve and enjoy.

Nutrition Facts

Calories 260

Fat 8g

Dietary Fiber 12g

Carbohydrates 9g

Protein 9g

Cherry Cinnamon Smoothie

Makes: 1 Serving

Ingredients:

1 apple, peeled and cored

1 ¼ cups almond milk

½ cup oats, soaked

½ cup cherries

Dash of cinnamon for taste

Directions:

The first thing you will need to do is place your oats in some water, enough to cover them, and let them soak overnight.

The next morning blend together all of your ingredients including the soaked oats and blend until smooth in consistency.

Pour smoothie into tall drinking glasses and adjust the taste by adding in cinnamon. Serve and enjoy.

Nutrition Facts

Calories 270

Fat 16g

Dietary Fiber 8g

Carbohydrates 15g

Protein 7g

Minty Blast Smoothie

This low carb smoothie recipe will not only leave you feeling healthy, but it will leave your entire body feeling refreshed as well. Made with fresh mint and parsley, this recipe is packed full of a minty taste that you will not be able to get enough of!

Makes: 1 Serving

Ingredients

1 avocado, peeled

1 kiwi, peeled

1 handful of mint, fresh

1 handful of spinach, fresh

1 handful of parsley, fresh

1 cup of water, filtered

Directions:

Place your avocado into a freezer and allow to sit until frozen completely.

Then place all of your ingredients into a blender. Blend together until smooth in consistency.

Pour into tall drinking glasses and add in ice. Serve immediately.

Nutrition Facts

Calories 246

Fat 15g

Dietary Fiber 7g

Carbohydrates 10g

Protein 8g

Blackberry Chia Smoothie

If you're looking for a smoothie recipe that is packed full of sweet taste, yet incredibly healthy, then this is the recipe for you. Using only the freshest berries possible, this is one smoothie recipe that you will want to make over and over again.

Makes: 1 Serving

Ingredients:

1 ½ cup almond milk, unsweetened

1/3 cup blueberries, fresh or frozen

1/3 cup blackberries, fresh or frozen

1 tbsp. chia seeds

1 handful of spinach, fresh

Directions:

If you are using fresh blueberries and blackberries, place them into your freezer to freeze for at least 3 hours.

After 3 hours remove the berries from the freezer and place into a blender with the rest of your ingredients. Blend everything together until smooth in consistency and transfer into a tall drinking glass. Enjoy immediately.

Nutrition Facts

Calories 235

Fat 5g

Dietary Fiber 6g

Carbohydrates 10g

Protein 7g

Emerald Detoxifier

As the name implies this is one of the best smoothie recipes to enjoy if you need to detoxify your body. While this smoothie is incredibly sweet, it packs a nutritional punch to boot.

Makes: 1 Serving

Ingredients:

1 grapefruit, peeled

2 cups of spinach

1 Granny Smith apple, peeled and cored

½ banana

1 handful of parsley, fresh

1 small chunk of ginger, peeled

1 cup water, filtered

3 to 4 ice cubes

Directions:

Using a blender, combine all of your ingredients together and blend until smooth.

If your smoothie is too thick in consistency, add in some ice cubes to reach desired consistency.

Transfer to a tall drinking glass and enjoy!

Nutrition Facts

Calories 180g

Fat 3g

Dietary Fiber 8g

Carbohydrates 8g

Protein 8g

Superfood Salad Smoothie

Makes: 1 Serving

Ingredients:

1 tomato, Roma

½ habanero pepper, seeds removed

½ cucumber

1 cup cabbage, white

1 lemon, fresh and juiced

1 handful of parsley, fresh and roughly torn

1 handful of kale, de-stemmed

½ cup water, filtered

5 to 6 ice cubes

Directions

Using a blender, blend all of your ingredients together until smooth in consistency.

If your smoothie is too thick, add in your ice cubes and blend again. Transfer to a tall drinking glass and enjoy!

Nutrition Facts

Calories 180

Fat 3g

Dietary Fiber 10g

Carbohydrates 4g

Protein 9g

Ginger and Pineapple Smoothie

Makes: 3 servings

Ingredients

1 cup pineapple, cubes

½ tablespoon of fresh ginger

1 cup of coconut milk

½ tablespoon of lemon juice

1 teaspoon of honey

1 tablespoon of mint leaves

6 Ice cubes, for chilling

Directions

Combine all the listed ingredients in a blender and pulse for about 30 seconds.

Once the desired consistency obtained, pour into serving glasses.

Nutrition Facts

Calories 223

Fat 19.2g

Dietary Fiber 2.8 g

Carbohydrates 14.4g

Protein 2.3g

Apple and Pecan Smoothie

Makes: 2 Servings

Ingredients

1 apple, with the skin left on

2 pieces of pecans, unsalted

1 tablespoon of soaked cashews

1 cup of water

4 ice cubes, for chilling

Pinch of cinnamon, or to taste

1/3 teaspoon of nutmeg

Directions

Blend all the listed ingredients in the blender for about 30 seconds.

Serve in ice-filled glasses and enjoy.

Nutrition Facts

Calories 81

Fat 3g

Dietary Fiber 2.5g

Carbohydrates 14.3g

Protein 1.0g

Strawberry Blueberry Smoothie

Makes: 2 Servings

Ingredients

½ cup strawberries, frozen

½ cup blueberries, frozen

½ cup plain yogurt

½ cup of water

Stevia, to taste (optional)

Ice cubes, for chilling

Directions

Blend all the ingredients together in a blender for 10-20 seconds.

Serve in tall serving glasses and enjoy.

Nutrition Facts

Calories 76

Fat 1 g

Dietary Fiber 1.6g

Carbohydrates 12.3g

Protein 4g

Apple Cinnamon Smoothie

Makes: 4 Servings

Ingredients

1 cup of pineapple

1 medium apple, de-seeded

1 cup almond milk

Pinch of cinnamon

6 ice cubes

½ cup of water

Ice cubes, for chilling

Directions

Blend all the ingredients together in a blender for 10-20 seconds.

Serve into tall serving glasses and enjoy.

Nutrition Facts

Calories 75

Fat 1.4g

Dietary Fiber 1.7g

Carbohydrates 14.8g

Protein 2.3 g

Matcha and Almond Smoothie

Makes: 2 Servings

Ingredients

2 cups of almond milk

1 tablespoon of crushed almonds

2 tablespoons of Matcha powder

Pinch of cinnamon

6 Ice cubes

Directions

Blend all the ingredients in your blender until smooth.

Pour into serving glasses.

Serve and enjoy.

Nutrition Facts

Calories 176

Fat 6.8g

Dietary Fiber 0.5g

Carbohydrates 12.8 g

Protein 10g

Matcha and Avocado Smoothie

Makes: 2 Servings

Ingredients

1 avocado, mashed

½ cup blueberries

1 cup filtered water

2 teaspoons of Matcha powder

Ice cubes, as needed

Directions

Blend all the ingredients together in a blender for 20-30 seconds.

Pour into tall serving glasses and enjoy.

Nutrition Facts

Calories 238

Fat 19.6g

Dietary Fiber 7.6g

Carbohydrates 13.9g

Protein 2.7g

Pineapple Blueberry Smoothie

Makes: 2 Servings

Ingredients

1 cup coconut milk

1/3 cup pineapples

¼ cup blueberries

1 tablespoon hemp seeds

3-4 ice cubes

Directions

Blend all the ingredients in a blender for 30-40 seconds.

Pour into tall glasses and enjoy.

Nutrition Facts

Calories 300

Fat 28.7g

Dietary Fiber 3.5g

Carbohydrates 12.9g

Protein 3 g

Strawberry Mint Smoothie

Makes: 1 Serving

Ingredients

2 cups water

1 cup strawberries, frozen

1/3 teaspoon cayenne pepper

1 tablespoon stevia

1 tablespoon of mint leaves

1 tablespoon Matcha powder

Few ice cubes

Directions

Toss all the ingredients into the blender.

Blend for 30 seconds until smooth and creamy.

Nutrition Facts

Calories 90

Fat 0.3g

Dietary Fiber 3.6 g

Carbohydrates 13.8g

Protein 1.7g

Metabolism Booster Smoothie

Makes: 2 Servings

Ingredients

1/4 teaspoon cayenne pepper

2 pinches of oregano

1 garlic clove

1 orange

1 cup water

1 apple (peeled and cored)

Directions

Place all the ingredients into your blender.

Blend for 30 seconds or until smooth and creamy.

Pour into tall glasses and enjoy.

Nutrition Facts

Calories 59

Fat 0.2g

Dietary Fiber 3.1g

Carbohydrates 14.6g

Protein 1.3g

Pomegranate Smoothie

Makes: 4-5 Servings

Ingredients

Seeds from 2 pomegranates

1 cup raspberries, frozen

1 cup pomegranate juice

1/3 teaspoon lemon juice

Pinch of salt

2 cups water

Directions

Place all the ingredients into your blender.

Blend for 30 seconds or until smooth and creamy.

Pour into tall glasses and enjoy.

Nutrition Facts

Calories 53

Fat 0.2 g

Dietary Fiber 2g

Carbohydrates 13.3g

Protein 0.7g

Instant Fat Fighter Smoothie

Makes: 4 Servings

Ingredients

1 tomato

½ teaspoon of cayenne pepper

1 cucumber

4 celery sticks

1 lemon, fresh and juiced

2 oz. of parsley, fresh

4 oz. kale, de-stemmed

2 cups water

5 to 6 ice cubes

Directions

Combine all the ingredients in a blender and pulse on high until smooth and creamy.

Add more ice cubes if the smoothie gets too thick.

Nutrition Facts

Calories 50

Fat 0.4 g

Dietary Fiber 3.1g

Carbohydrates 10.3 g

Protein 2.6 g

high protein low carb Smoothies

Vanilla Heaven Smoothie

This creamy and white smoothie is sweet in taste and one of the most delicious low carb smoothies around. Perfect after a long workout!

Makes: 1 Serving

Ingredients

1 ¾ cup coconut milk, unsweetened

¼ cup of protein powder, vanilla flavored

½ tsp. of vanilla extract

Directions:

Place all of your ingredients together into a blend. Pulse your ingredients until they are smooth in consistency.

If your smoothie is too thick, add in your ice cubes and continue to pulse until smooth in consistency. Transfer to a tall drinking glass and serve immediately.

Nutrition Facts

Calories 212

Fat 5g

Dietary Fiber 2g

Carbohydrates 12g

Protein 5g

Almond Pineapple Smoothie

If you are looking for a low carb healthy smoothie recipe, but want to build some lean muscles in the process; this is a great recipe to try. Low in carbs and packed full of protein, this is the tasty recipe that will help get you into shape.

Makes: 1 Serving

Ingredients

2/3 cup almond milk, unsweetened

1/3 cup pineapple, chopped

10 almonds

2 tbsp. low carb protein powder

Directions:

Combine all the ingredients together in a blender and blend until smooth in consistency. Pour into a tall drinking glass and top with ice cubes. Enjoy!

Nutrition Facts

Calories 320

Fat 5g

Dietary Fiber 13g

Carbohydrates 9g

Protein 15g

Chocolate Peanut Butter Smoothie

This is a great smoothie recipe to put together if you are looking to enjoy a sweet tasting chocolaty snack. Packed full of nutritional benefits, this is certainly one smoothie recipe that you will have no problem enjoying.

Makes: 1 Serving

Ingredients:

1 cup almond milk, unsweetened

2 tbsp. peanut butter, natural and unsweetened

2 tbsp. cocoa powder, unsweetened

3 to 4 tbsp. whey protein powder, vanilla flavored

2 tbsp. heavy whipping cream

¼ tsp. of vanilla extract

2 cups of ice

Directions

Add in your milk and ice into a blender first. Then add the rest of your ingredients into the blender next. Blend everything together until smooth in consistency. Transfer into a tall drinking glass and enjoy!

Nutrition Facts

Calories 360

Fat 17g

Dietary Fiber 3g

Carbohydrates 9g

Protein 12g

Avocado Almond Smoothie

Makes: 1 Serving

Ingredients

2 cups spinach, fresh

1 cup almond milk

½ avocado, pits removed

¼ cup protein powder, vanilla flavored

1½ cups of ice

Directions:

Chop up your avocado and place in a blender. Add in the rest of your ingredients and blend until smooth in consistency. Transfer into a tall drinking glass and enjoy immediately.

Nutrition Facts

Calories 280g

Fat 15g

Dietary Fiber 8g

Carbohydrates 11g

Protein 8g

Blueberry Spinach Smoothie

Makes: 1 Serving

Ingredients:

1 cup almond milk, unsweetened

3 tbsp. oats (soaked overnight)

¾ cups of Greek yogurt, plain

1 ½ cups blueberries

3 cups spinach,

1 ½ cups of ice, crushed

Directions:

The first thing you will need to do is place your blueberries into the freezer. Let them sit until they are completely frozen.

Blend together all of your ingredients including the soaked oats and blend until smooth in consistency. Pour smoothie into tall drinking glasses. Serve and enjoy.

Nutrition Facts

Calories 272

Fat 12g

Dietary Fiber 8g

Carbohydrates 9g

Protein 10g

Almond Cinnamon Smoothie

Makes: 1 Serving

Ingredients:

1 cup almond milk

2 tbsp. protein powder

¼ tsp. vanilla extract

1 tbsp. flax meal

1 tbsp. hemp seeds

1 cup of ice

Dash of cinnamon for taste

Directions:

Add all of your ingredients into a blender and blend until the entire mixture is smooth in consistency. Pour your freshly made smoothie mixture into tall drinking glasses and garnish with a dash of cinnamon. Serve and enjoy.

Nutrition Facts

Calories 320

Fat 12g

Dietary Fiber 8g

Carbohydrates 11g

Protein 14g

Polka Dot Smoothie

Makes: 2 Servings

Ingredients

1/3 cup of coconut milk

1 cup spinach, fresh

1/3 cup blueberries, frozen

1/4 cup blackberries, frozen

1/3 tablespoon of chia seeds

A scoop of low carb protein powder

4 Ice cubes

Directions

Pulse all the ingredients in your blender.

Blend until smooth or desired consistency is obtained.

Pour into ice-filled glasses and enjoy.

Nutrition Facts

Calories 188

Fat 11.5 g

Dietary Fiber 3.7 g

Carbohydrates 10 g

Protein 13.4g

Almond Butter Smoothie

Makes: 2 Servings

Ingredients

1 cup almond milk

1 scoop protein powder (low carb)

2 tablespoons almond butter

12 almonds, sliced

Pinch of cinnamon

4 ice cubes

Directions

Pour all the ingredients into a high-speed blender and process until you reach the desired consistency. Serve in ice-filled glasses and enjoy.

Nutrition Facts

Calories 225

Fat 14.7 g

Dietary Fiber 1.6g

Carbohydrates 12.4 g

Protein 20.1 g

High Power Smoothie

Makes: 2 Servings

Ingredients

1 cup coconut milk

2 scoops of whey protein

2 organic eggs

1 tablespoon almond butter

12 almonds

4 ice cubes, for chilling

Directions

Pour all the ingredients into a high-speed blender and process until you reach the desired consistency. Serve and enjoy chilled.

Nutrition Facts

Calories 551

Fat 30.8g

Dietary Fiber 3.8 g

Carbohydrates 13.6g

Protein 33.6g

Chocolate and Peanut Smoothie

Makes: 2-3 Servings

Ingredients

1 cup almond milk

2 oz. peanuts, natural, non-salted

2 tablespoons of cocoa powder

1 tablespoon of flax seeds

2 scoops of low carb protein powder

2 cups of ice

Directions

Blend all the ingredients in a high speed blender. Serve in ice-filled glasses and enjoy.

Nutrition Facts

Calories 248

Fat 13.4g

Dietary Fiber 3.3 g

Carbohydrates 12.1 g

Protein 23.4 g

Spinach Avocado Smoothie

Makes: 6 Servings

Ingredients

2 oz. spinach, fresh

2 cups coconut milk

2 avocados, pits removed

4 scoops of protein powder, vanilla flavored

1 cup of ice

2 tablespoons of almond butter

1-2 cups water

Directions

Place all the ingredients in a blender and pulse until smooth.

Pour into ice-filled glasses and serve.

Nutrition Facts

Calories 477

Fat 37g

Dietary Fiber 6.7g

Carbohydrates 14.9 g

Protein 26.6 g

Blueberry Power Protein Smoothie

Makes: 2-3 Servings

Ingredients

2 scoops of protein powder

2 tablespoons of organic coconut oil

1 cup blueberries

1 cup coconut milk

1 teaspoon almond butter

1 apple (peeled and cored)

1 cup ice

Directions

Add all the ingredients to a blender and blend for 40 seconds or until smooth.

Serve in a tall glass and enjoy.

Nutrition Facts

Calories 292

Fat 18.8 g

Dietary Fiber 2.7 g

Carbohydrates 14.9g

Protein 19.2g

Pure Protein Smoothie

Makes: 4 Servings

Ingredients

2 scoops of whey protein

1 cup blueberries

1 cup coconut milk

1 teaspoon of cocoa, unsweetened

4 tablespoons of flaxseed

Ice cubes for chilling

Directions

Blend all the ingredients together in a blender. Serve in ice-filled glasses and enjoy.

Nutrition Facts

Calories 257

Fat 15g

Dietary Fiber 4.2g

Carbohydrates 12.7g

Protein 14.1g

Apple Protein Smoothie

Makes: 8 servings

Ingredients

2 apples, skin and seeds removed

2 cups almond milk

1-ounce almonds (raw)

6 scoops of protein powder (low carb)

Pinch of cinnamon

½ teaspoons of nutmeg

4 or 5 ice cubes

Directions

Blend all the ingredients together in a blender.

Serve in ice-filled glasses and enjoy.

Nutrition Facts

Calories 165

Fat 4.5g

Dietary Fiber 1.6g

Carbohydrates 12.8g

Protein 19.5g

energizing

low carb Smoothies

Sunshine Smoothie

Makes: 4 Servings

Ingredients

1 cup coconut milk

1/3 cup of soaked oats

½ apple, de-cored

½ cup orange, juice

¼ teaspoon cinnamon

12 almonds, sliced

2 cups ice cubes, for chilling

Directions

Blend the above ingredients in a high-speed blender.

Serve in ice-filled glasses and enjoy.

Nutrition Facts

Calories 207

Fat 16.6 g

Dietary Fiber 3.6 g

Carbohydrates 14.6g

Protein 3.3 g

Coffee Lover Smoothie

If you are trying to avoid drinking coffee and are looking for a healthier alternative, this is the recipe for you. This smoothie will give you the energy you need to wake you up in the morning and satisfy you at the same time.

Makes: 1 Serving

Ingredients:

2 tbsp. coffee, powder

3 to 4 tbsp. protein powder, vanilla flavored

½ cup coconut milk

2 tbsp. flaxseed meal

1 cup of water

Directions:

Using a glass mix your coffee powder with at least a cup of cold water. Then pour your coffee into a large sized shaker along with the rest of your ingredients.

Shake your ingredients thoroughly together. Pour your mixture into a tall drinking glass and top with a few ice cubes. Serve and enjoy immediately.

Nutrition Facts

Calories 356

Fat 12g

Dietary Fiber 14g

Carbohydrates 11g

Protein 15g

Berry-licious Blast Smoothie

Makes: 1 Serving

Ingredients:

½ cup raspberries, fresh

½ cup strawberries, fresh

½ cup blackberries, fresh

1 cup almond milk

A few ice cubes

Directions:

Using a blender, mix together all of your berries. Then add in your milk and blend everything until the mixture is smooth in consistency.

If your mixture is too thick, add in a few ices cubes. Continue blending until the consistency is perfect for you. Pour into tall drinking glass and serve at once.

Nutrition Facts

Calories 150

Fat 1g

Dietary Fiber 12g

Carbohydrates 9g

Protein 7g

Avocado Coconut Smoothie

Makes: 1 Serving

Ingredients:

½ avocado, fresh

2 oz. cashews

1 tbsp. of coconut oil

1 cup water

1 cup coconut milk

A few coconut flakes

Directions:

Place your avocado into your blender then add in the rest of your ingredients and blend until smooth in consistency.

Pour into a tall drinking glass and garnish with colored coconut flakes. Enjoy!

Nutrition Facts

Calories 193

Fat 7g

Dietary Fiber 3g

Carbohydrates 8g

Protein 7g

Egg and Melon Smoothie

The best way to make your smoothie a meal replacer is to add organic eggs to it. Organic eggs will add a creamy texture and provide you with a source of complete protein. In addition, you will hardly notice the taste!

Makes: 1 Serving

Ingredients

1 organic egg, beaten lightly

½ cup melon, fresh

1 tsp. sesame oil

½ tsp. vanilla

1 cup almond milk

Directions

First beat your egg lightly until it begins to foam slightly. Add in your chopped fresh melon and the remaining ingredients. Blend everything together until evenly combined. Pour into a glass and serve.

Nutrition Facts

Calories 190

Fat 15g

Dietary Fiber 13g

Carbohydrates 8g

Protein 14g

Morella Cherry Smoothie

Unlike many low carb smoothie recipes, you will not find one that is as delicious as this one. Packed full of cherry flavor that you love, you can enjoy this sweet tasting recipe while giving your body all of the nutrients that it needs.

Makes: 1 Serving

Ingredients:

1/3 cup Greek yogurt, plain

1 cup Morella Cherries, stems and pits removed

1 tbsp. chia seeds

1 cup almond milk

1 cup spinach

Directions:

Wash your cherries and remove the pits. Place your washed and pitted cherries into a blender along with your yogurt. Blend until your mixture is smooth in consistency.

Nutrition Facts

Calories 165

Fat 8g

Dietary Fiber 9g

Carbohydrates 9g

Protein 5.8g

Raspberry Dream Smoothie

Raspberries, spinach and peppers make this smoothie an antioxidant powerhouse. This smoothie is also incredibly high in vitamin C, E, beta-carotene and fiber.

Makes 1 serving.

Ingredients:

1 cup spinach (chopped)

½ raspberries (fresh or frozen)

1 Roma tomato

8 oz. cold filtered water

½ red bell pepper

6 medium strawberries

Few ice cubes

Directions:

Wash fruits and vegetables thoroughly. Remove stems and seeds. Add all the ingredients to a high speed blender and blend on high until you reach a smooth and creamy consistency, approximately 1 minute.

Nutrition Facts

Calories 125

Fat 1g

Dietary Fiber 4g

Carbohydrates 10g

Protein 5g

Kale Cherry Booster Smoothie

This smoothie is packed with antioxidants and nutrients, which protect against heart disease, boost your immune system and assist the kidneys and liver in eliminating harmful toxins.

Makes 1-2 servings.

Ingredients:

1 cup frozen cherries

1 cup kale, stems removed

1 cup filtered water

2 tbsp. hemp seeds

1 cup ice

1 tbsp. organic coconut oil

Directions:

Add all the ingredients to a high speed blender and blend on high until you reach a smooth and creamy consistency, approximately 1 minute.

Nutrition Facts

Calories 147

Fat 9g

Dietary Fiber 9g

Carbohydrates 8.5g

Protein 15.6g

Blueberry Almond Power Smoothie

This smoothie is sure to provide you with a burst of energy and is a great choice for breakfast. It's packed with healthy fats in the form of coconut oil, nut butter and avocado, great for boosting brain power.

Makes 1-2 servings.

Ingredients:

1 small avocado (skin and pit removed)

1 tbsp. organic coconut oil

1 cup blueberries

1 cup coconut milk

1 tbsp. almond butter

1 apple (cored and diced)

1 cup ice

Directions:

Add all the ingredients to a blender and blend for 1-2 minutes or until smooth.

Nutrition Facts

Calories 260

Fat 12g

Dietary Fiber 30g

Carbohydrates 14g

Protein 15g

Berries and Spinach Smoothie

Makes: 2 Servings

Ingredients

1 cup coconut milk, unsweetened

1 cup of yogurt, plain

1 cup blueberries (frozen)

1 cup raspberries

2 cups spinach

1 cup crushed ice

Directions

Combine the listed ingredients in a blender and pulse until smooth.

Pour into the ice-filled glasses and serve.

Nutrition Facts

Calories 148

Fat 10.3g

Dietary Fiber 3g

Carbohydrates 11.4g

Protein 4g

Berries Medley

Makes: 2 Servings

Ingredients

1 cup of yogurt, plain

1 cup blueberries (frozen)

1 cup raspberries

1 cup of blackberries

1 cup of strawberries

1 cup water

Crushed ice for chilling

Directions

Combine the above ingredients in a blender and pulse until smooth and creamy.

Nutrition Facts

Calories 78

Fat 0.9 g

Dietary Fiber 3.6g

Carbohydrates 14.3g

Protein 2.9g

Orange Smoothie

Makes: 5 Servings

Ingredients

2 oranges, peeled

2 carrots, peeled and chopped

1 cup water

1 cup pineapple (frozen)

1 lemon, juiced

Ice cubes, for chilling

Directions

Combine all the listed ingredients in a high speed blender and pulse until smooth and creamy. Serve in ice-filled glasses and enjoy.

Nutrition Facts

Calories 53

Fat 0.1 g

Dietary Fiber 2.4 g

Carbohydrates 13.4 g

Protein 0.9 g

Coffee Flavored Smoothie

Makes: 4 Servings

Ingredients

2 tablespoons of coffee, powder

4 tablespoons of protein powder, vanilla flavored

2 cups coconut milk

1 tablespoon flaxseed meal

1/2 cup water

Directions

Take a small bowl and mix coffee with half cup of water.

Pour the coffee into the blender and add the rest of the ingredients.

Once smoothie is prepared, pour into ice-filled glasses and enjoy.

Nutrition Facts

Calories 405

Fat 31 g

Dietary Fiber 3.1g

Carbohydrates 10g

Protein 25.5g

Tropical Berry Smoothie

Makes: 2 Servings

Ingredients

1 cup mango (frozen)

1 cup raspberries

2 teaspoons honey

1 cup coconut milk

Directions

Combine the above ingredients in a blender and pulse until smooth.

Pour the smoothie into ice-filled glasses and serve.

Best served chilled.

Nutrition Facts

Calories 114

Fat 21 g

Dietary Fiber 5.1 g

Carbohydrates 12.9g

Protein 24 g

Soy Protein Smoothie

Makes: 3 Servings

Ingredients

2 cups almond milk

2 scoops soy protein powder

1 cup raspberries

20 almonds

4 cup ice cubes

Directions

Combine all the above ingredients in a high speed blender and pulse until smooth.

Pour the smoothie into ice-filled glasses and serve.

Nutrition Facts

Calories 215

Fat 8.3 g

Dietary Fiber 2.8 g

Carbohydrates 13.1 g

Protein 23.8 g

Non-Dairy Strawberry Smoothie

Makes: 1 Serving

Ingredients

2 cups strawberries

1 cup spinach

1 tablespoon chia seeds

2 cups coconut water

4 ice cubes

2 teaspoons of raw honey

Directions

Combine all the above ingredients in a blender and pulse until smooth.

Pour the smoothie into ice-filled glasses and serve.

Nutrition Facts

Calories 113

Fat 0 g

Dietary Fiber 0g

Carbohydrates 11.5 g

Protein 0.0g

Banana, Mint, and Basil Smoothie

Makes: 2 Servings

Ingredients

2 bananas, peeled

1 cup mixed frozen berries

10 basil leaves, fresh

1 tablespoon honey

2 cups filtered water

4 mint leaves

Directions

Combine all the above ingredients in a blender and pulse until smooth.

Pour the smoothie into ice-filled glasses and serve.

Nutrition Facts

Calories 46

Fat 0.1g

Dietary Fiber 1g

Carbohydrates 11.9 g

Protein 0.5g

Mango, Banana, and Strawberry Smoothie

Makes: 2-4 Servings

Ingredients

1 mango, peeled, pitted and cubed

1 cup orange juice, fresh

½ tablespoon of lime juice

1 cup water

4 ice cubes

Top Layer ingredients

1 banana, chopped

6 strawberries cut in half

2 Ice cubes

1 cup water

Directions

Take a blender and pulse mango, orange juice, honey, lime juice along with ice cubes. Divide the liquid amongst the glasses and set aside.

Rinse the blender and then add all the top layer ingredients. Pulse for 20 seconds on low speed and then pour into the half- filled glasses.

Nutrition Facts

Calories 58

Fat 0.2g

Dietary Fiber 1.3g

Carbohydrates 14.2g

Protein 0.8g

Fruit and Veggie Smoothie

Makes: 2-4 Servings

Ingredients

4 apples, peeled and seeded

2 cups fresh pineapples, cut and cubed

1 cup coconut water

1 cup ice

1 teaspoon lemon juice

1 cup beetroot, peeled and chopped

2 cups celery sticks

Directions

Combine the above ingredients in a high-speed blender and pulse. Best served chilled.

Nutrition Facts

Calories 68

Fat 0.2g

Dietary Fiber 2.8 g

Carbohydrates 15.1g

Protein 0.7g

Kiwi Goodness Smoothie

Makes: 3 Servings

Ingredients

1 avocado, frozen and peeled

1 oz. mint leaves, fresh

2 oz. spinach leaves

1 handful fresh parsley

2 kiwis, peeled

2 cups of ice cubes

Directions

Blend all the above ingredients in a blender.

Serve in ice-filled glasses and enjoy.

Nutrition Facts

Calories 179

Fat 13.5 g

Dietary Fiber 7.1g

Carbohydrates 14.7g

Protein 2.7g

breakfast

low carb Smoothies

Cocoa Macadamia Smoothie

This smoothie is sure to give your taste buds a treat! It's also loaded with healthy fats that will keep you full and satisfied for hours.

Makes 1 serving.

Ingredients:

Stevia to taste

½ tsp. vanilla extract

2 tbsp. macadamia nuts (crushed)

1 tbsp. unsweetened cocoa powder

¾ cup coconut milk

1 cup ice cubes

Dash of salt

Directions:

Add all the ingredients to a high speed blender and blend on high until smooth.

Nutrition Facts

Calories 357

Fat 12g

Dietary fiber 7g

Net carbohydrates 12g

Protein 16g

Strawberries and Cream Smoothie

This is a classic flavor combination that is delicious and creamy thanks to the avocado and cashews. The hemp seeds provide a mega dose of omega-3 fatty acids. Enjoy!

Makes 1 serving.

Ingredients:

1 tbsp. raw cashews

1 cup frozen strawberries

1 cup coconut milk

1 medium avocado (peeled and cored)

1 tbsp. hemp hearts

Stevia to taste

Directions:

Add all the ingredients to a high speed blender and blend on high until smooth.

Nutrition Facts

Calories 312

Fat 58g

Dietary Fiber 22g

Net carbohydrates 10g

Protein 20g

Chocolate Raspberry Smoothie

Nothing beats the combination of chocolate and raspberries. Raspberries and cocoa powder provide a healthy dose of antioxidants and bananas add soluble fiber to keep your digestive system working all day long.

Makes: 1 serving.

Ingredients:

1/3 cup soaked cashews

2 tbsp. cocoa power (unsweetened)

½ avocado

1 cup raspberries (fresh or frozen)

1 cup almond milk

1 cup ice

Directions:

Add all the ingredients to a high speed blender and blend on high until smooth.

Nutrition Facts

Calories 115

Fat 15g

Dietary Fiber 5g

Net carbohydrates 8g

Protein 12g

Berry Mint Smoothie

This delicious creation is highlighted by the freshness of mint and the tartness of berries. Enjoy on a warm summer day!

Makes: 1-2 smoothies

Ingredients:

1 cup almond milk

1 cup coconut milk

1 cup frozen blueberries

1 cup frozen raspberries

1 tbsp. organic coconut oil

½ cup mint leaves (fresh)

½ lemon juice

Stevia or other sweetener to taste

Directions:

Add all the ingredients to a high speed blender and blend on high until smooth.

Nutrition Facts

Calories 286

Fat 8g

Dietary Fiber 4g

Net carbohydrates 12g

Protein 12g

Strawberry Raspberry Bliss Smoothie

This is a simple yet delicious low carb treat! Studies show that people who consume as little as 2 ounces of almonds daily, develop better insulin sensitivity and lower their cholesterol. Strawberries are high in antioxidants and protect cells against free radical damage.

Makes 1 serving.

Ingredients:

½ cup raw almonds (soaked overnight)

1 cup organic strawberries (frozen)

1 cup filtered water

½ cup organic raspberries (frozen)

Stevia to taste

Directions:

Blend the almonds and water until creamy. Add the rest of the ingredients to a high speed blender and blend on high until smooth.

Nutrition Facts

Calories 210

Fat 8g

Dietary Fiber 4g

Net carbohydrates 10g

Protein 4g

Mango & Peach Surprise

The combination of nuts and seeds in this smoothie make it dense in protein, good fats, and energy: everything you need to get through a busy, active morning.

Makes 1 serving.

Ingredients:

½ cup mango (diced, frozen)

½ cup peach (diced, frozen)

¼ cup pumpkin seeds

¼ cup almonds

¼ cup hemp seeds

2 cups almond milk

½ teaspoon vanilla extract

Directions:

Combine ingredients in a blender and blend on high for 1 minute or until smooth.

Nutrition Facts

Calories 130

Fat 13g

Dietary Fiber 10g

Carbohydrates 9g

Protein 6g

Apple-licious Banana n' Nuts

The relatively high fat content of this smoothie prevents it from being an everyday staple, but it could be an especially apt choice before an intense workout or in anticipation of a late lunch.

Makes 1-2 servings.

Ingredients:

½ apple (peeled and diced)

½ banana

2 cups coconut milk

½ cup walnuts

½ cup macadamia

½ tsp. nutmeg

½ tsp. cinnamon

½ cup of ice (optional)

Directions:

Combine ingredients in a blender and blend on high for 1 minute or until smooth.

Nutrition Facts Per Serving:

Calories 215

Fat 16g

Dietary Fiber 16g

Net carbohydrates 14g

Protein 16g

Green Breakfast Smoothie

Makes 2 smoothies.

Ingredients:

1 cup coconut water

1 tbsp. almond butter

¼ cup wheat grass

2 cups spinach leaves

1 scoop low carb chocolate protein (ex. Designer Protein)

1 inch slice of banana

Pinch of Stevia

½ cup ice

Directions:

Combine the listed ingredients into a high-speed blender. Blend everything on high for an entire minute. The individual pieces of spinach should disappear. The smoothie should be incredibly green—ready for your low-carb grab and go breakfast snack.

Nutrition Facts Per Serving:

Calories 155

Fat 4g

Dietary Fiber 2g

Net carbohydrates 3g

Protein 15g

Berry Breakfast Low Carb Smoothie

Makes 2 smoothies.

Ingredients:

1 cup cold coffee

1 scoop low carb vanilla protein powder

½ cup coconut milk

2 tbsp. flax seed meal

½ cup blueberries

2 tbsp. blackberries

Pinch of Stevia

4 ice cubes

Directions:

Place all the ingredients into your high-speed blender and blend for one minute. Enjoy your protein-rich, energy-driven breakfast smoothie.

Nutrition Facts Per Serving:

Calories 141

Fat 12g

Dietary Fiber 2g

Net carbohydrates 7g

Protein 23g

Strawberry Splash Breakfast Smoothie

Makes 2 smoothies.

Ingredients:

8 large strawberries

2 cups almond milk (unsweetened)

12 ice cubes

1 cup Greek yogurt (plain with whole milk)

Directions:

Place the de-stemmed strawberries, soy milk, yogurt, and ice cubes into your blender. Blend on high until smooth, approximately 2 minutes. Enjoy your low-carb morning!

Nutrition Facts Per Serving:

Calories 161

Fat 9g

Dietary Fiber 2g

Net carbohydrates 11g

Protein 13g

Pumpkin Spice Smoothie

Makes: 1 Serving.

Ingredients:

¾ cup almond milk, unsweetened

¼ cup heavy cream

¼ cup pumpkin puree

2 Tbsp. of Stevia

¼ tsp. of Pumpkin Pie Spice

Directions:

Add in all of your ingredients into a blender and blend until smooth in consistency.

Pour into a tall drinking glass. Serve chilled. Enjoy!

Nutrition Facts Per Serving

Calories 193

Fat 16g

Dietary Fiber 12g

Carbohydrates 3g

Protein 11.3g

Sweet and Creamy Chocolate Smoothie

Makes: 1 Serving

Ingredients:

1 cup almond milk, unsweetened

½ banana

½ avocado

2 tbsp. cacao, raw, unsweetened

2 tbsp. almond butter

½ cup ice

1 ½ tsp. flaxseed

Directions:

Add in all of your ingredients into a high speed blender and blend thoroughly together until the mixture is smooth in consistency. Pour into a drinking glass and enjoy immediately.

Nutrition Facts Per Serving

Calories 125

Fat 9g

Dietary Fiber 2g

Net carbohydrates 14g

Protein 18g

Cappuccino Egg Cream Low Carb Smoothie

Makes 1 smoothie.

Ingredients:

1 cup cold coffee

2 tbsp. cream

2 organic eggs

4 tbsp. cinnamon flavored sugar-free syrup

3 ice cubes

Directions:

Toss your cup of cold coffee, cream, two eggs, sugar-free syrup, and your ice cubes into a blender. Blend on high speed until your drink is smooth. You can add a bit of Stevia to taste, if you have a special sweet tooth in the morning.

Nutrition Facts Per Serving:

Calories 220

Fat 9g

Dietary Fiber 2g

Net carbohydrates 7g

Protein 13g

Strawberry Tofu Power Smoothie

Makes 2-3 Smoothies.

Ingredients

1 cup frozen strawberries

1 cup ice cubes

1 cup ice water

½ cup heavy cream

1 tsp. Splenda

3 ½ ounces tofu

½ tsp. vanilla

Directions:

Toss all the ingredients: strawberries, ice cubes, water, cream, Splenda, tofu, and the vanilla into a blender. Set the blender to high and let it blend for a minute and a half. The mixture should be smooth. Separate the smoothie into four equal distributions.

Nutrition Facts Per Serving:

Calories 164

Fat 12g

Net carbohydrates 5g

Protein 4g

green

low carb Smoothies

Go Green Smoothie

Makes: 8 Servings

Ingredients

4 apples, peeled, de-seeded

4 sticks of celery

2 cucumbers (peeled)

2 cups ice

3 cups water

Directions

Wash the vegetables and fruit well before making the smoothie.

Combine all the ingredients in a blender and blend for 30 seconds.

Once smoothie is prepared, pour into serving glasses.

Nutrition Facts

Calories 61

Fat 0.3 g

Dietary Fiber 2.8 g

Carbohydrates 15.7 g

Protein 0.8 g

Power-up Punch

Makes: 4-6 Servings

Ingredients

10 celery sticks

1 avocado (pit removed)

2 green apples (cored)

1 cucumber

1 orange, juiced

1 lime, juiced

2 cups water

Directions

Wash the vegetables and fruit well before making the smoothie. Combine celery sticks, spinach, apples, cucumber, orange juice and lime juice in a high speed blender. Add a bit of water to make the consistency runny. Pulse for a few seconds and serve in ice-filled glasses.

Nutrition Facts

Calories 95

Fat 5.1 g

Dietary Fiber 3.9 g

Carbohydrates 13.4g

Protein 1.3 g

Green Goddess Smoothie

Makes: 3-4 Servings

Ingredients

½ cup green grapes

2 kiwis

1 lime, juice

1 cucumber, cubed

1 cup orange, juiced

1 cup ice cubes

Directions

Wash, chop and de-seed the fruits.

Blend all the above ingredients in a high speed blender until smooth and creamy and serve in ice-filled glasses.

Nutrition Facts

Calories 63

Fat 0.4g

Dietary Fiber 2.7 g

Carbohydrates 15 g

Protein 1.4g

Spinach and Cucumber Smoothie

Makes: 4 Servings

Ingredients

1 carrot, juiced

1 cucumber

1 small parsley bunch

1 bunch of spinach

1 bunch kale

2 lime, juiced

1-2 cup water

Directions

Wash the vegetables well before making the smoothie.

Blend all the ingredients in a blender until smooth and creamy.

Serve in ice-filled glasses and enjoy.

Nutrition Facts

Calories 76

Fat 1 g

Dietary Fiber 5.3 g

Carbohydrates 10.4 g

Protein 5.7g

Green Salad Smoothie

Makes: 2 Servings

Ingredients

1 habanero pepper, seeds removed
1 cucumber
2 cups cabbage, white
1 lemon, fresh and juiced
1 handful of parsley, fresh
2 mint leaves
½ handful of kale, de-stemmed
1 cup water, filtered
5 to 6 ice cubes

Directions

Wash the vegetables well before making the smoothie. Combine all the listed ingredients together in a blender and pulse until smooth and creamy. Once smooth consistency is obtained, pour into serving glasses and enjoy this refreshing drink.

Nutrition Facts

Calories 54

Fat 0.5 g

Dietary Fiber 4.1 g

Carbohydrates 11.8 g

Protein 3.1 g

Kale Madness

Makes: 4 Servings

Ingredients

4 cups kale, washed and chopped

2 cups orange juice, freshly squeezed

1 teaspoon lemon zest

1 cup water

1 cup ice cubes

Directions

Combine all the listed ingredients in a high speed blender. Pulse for about 30-45 seconds.

Nutrition Facts

Calories 60

Fat 0.2 g

Dietary Fiber 0.9 g

Carbohydrates 13.3 g

Protein 1.9 g

Natural Energizer Smoothie

Makes: 4 Servings

Ingredients

1 cup pineapple

2 cups spinach

1 cucumber

1 lime, juiced

1 cup ice cubes

1 cup of celery, chopped

1 cup fennel

Directions

Wash the fruits and vegetables well before making the smoothie. Combine all the listed ingredients in a high speed blender and pulse for about 30 seconds. Once the smoothie is prepared, pour into ice-filled glasses and enjoy.

Nutrition Facts

Calories 48

Fat 0.3g

Dietary Fiber 2.4g

Carbohydrates 11.9g

Protein 1.6g

Green AC Booster

Makes: 2-3 Servings

Ingredients

2 cups spinach, washed

4 large cucumbers

1/2 cup broccoli

1 cup kale

2 avocados, mashed

1 teaspoon of lemon juice

Ice cubes for chilling

1 cup water

Directions

Wash the vegetables well before making a smoothie. Combine all the listed ingredients in a high speed blender and pulse for about 30 seconds. Pour into ice-filled glasses and enjoy.

Nutrition Facts

Calories 177

Fat 13.4 g

Dietary Fiber 6.1g

Carbohydrates 14.8g

Protein 3.4 g

Cool Cucumber Smoothie

Makes: 4 Servings

Ingredients

4 cucumbers

2 limes, squeezed

Pinch of sea salt

Pinch of black pepper

½ teaspoon of ginger

ice cubes for chilling

Directions

Wash the cucumbers well before making the smoothie.

Place all the listed ingredients in a blender and pulse for 30 seconds.

Serve the smoothie in ice -filled glasses and enjoy.

Nutrition Facts

Calories 56

Fat 0.4 g

Dietary Fiber 2.5g

Carbohydrates 14.6g

Protein 2.2g

Fresh Herbs Smoothie

Makes: 2-3 servings

Ingredients

1 avocado, frozen and peeled

2 kiwis, peeled

1 handful of mint, fresh

1 handful of basil

1 handful of parsley

1 cup of water, filtered

Directions

Wash the vegetables, herbs and fruit well before making the smoothie. Combine ingredients into a blender and blend for 30 seconds. Pour into tall drinking glasses and add the ice. Serve chilled.

Nutrition Facts

Calories 177

Fat 13.5g

Dietary Fiber 7.1g

Carbohydrates 14.8g

Protein 2.8g

Avocado Powerhouse

Makes: 2-3 Servings

Ingredients

1 avocado, fresh

1 cup kale (de-stemmed)

1 cup spinach

1 tbsp. of coconut oil

1 cup water

1 cup coconut milk

A few coconut flakes

Few Ice cubes, for chilling

Directions

Wash the avocado well before making the smoothie. Combine all the ingredients in your blender, and then blend until smooth. Pour into ice-filled drinking glasses and garnish with coconut flakes. Serve and enjoy chilled.

Nutrition Facts

Calories 193

Fat 7g

Dietary Fiber 3g

Carbohydrates 4.5g

Protein 7g

Green Detoxifier Smoothie

Makes: 4-6 Servings

Ingredients

1 grapefruit, peeled

1 cup of spinach

1 cup kale, washed

1 green apple, peeled and cored

½ banana

1 handful of mint, fresh

1 ginger, peeled

1 cup water, filtered

3 to 4 ice cubes

Directions

Combine all of your ingredients together in a high-speed blender and blend until smooth. If your smoothie is too thick, add some ice cubes to reach desired consistency. Transfer to ice-filled glasses and enjoy.

Nutrition Facts

Calories 56g

Fat 0.4g

Dietary Fiber 2.4g

Carbohydrates 13.2g

Protein 1.4g

Green Pineapple Paradise

Makes: 2 Servings

Ingredients

1 cup water

1 cup pineapple

1 green apple

1 cup grapes

1 cup spinach

1 avocado

1 cup broccoli, cubed

1 cup water, filtered

3 to 4 ice cubes

Directions

Wash all fruits and vegetables well. Combine all of your ingredients together and blend until smooth. If your smoothie is too thick, add some ice cubes to reach desired consistency. Transfer to ice-filled glasses and enjoy.

Nutrition Facts

Calories 114g

Fat 6.7 g

Dietary Fiber 4g

Carbohydrates 14.5g

Protein 1.5 g

Tropical Blast

Makes: 2-4 Servings

Ingredients

1 cup fresh spinach

1 cup coconut water, unsweetened

1 orange, peeled

1 mango, frozen

½ cup pineapple, frozen

Juice of 1/2 lime

Directions

Combine all of your ingredients in a high speed blender. Blend for 30 seconds or until smooth in consistency. Pour into tall drinking glasses and add ice. Serve chilled.

Nutrition Facts

Calories 57

Fat 0.2g

Dietary Fiber 1.7g

Carbohydrates 14g

Protein 0.7g

Energizing Smoothie

Makes: 1 Serving

Ingredients

1 cup fresh spinach

½ cup coconut water, unsweetened

1 cup pineapple, frozen

Directions

Place all of your ingredients in a blender and blend for 30 seconds or until smooth. Pour into tall drinking glasses and add ice. Serve chilled.

Nutrition Facts

Calories 64

Fat 0.2 g

Dietary Fiber 1.5g

Carbohydrates 11.4 g

Protein 0.9g

Shamrock Green Smoothie

Makes: 4 Servings

Ingredients

2 cups coconut milk, unsweetened

1 cup fresh spinach

1/3 cup fresh mint leaves

1 banana, peeled

2 Medjool dates, pitted

Directions

Combine all of your ingredients in a blender and blend for 30 seconds. Pour into tall drinking glasses and add ice. Serve chilled.

Nutrition Facts

Calories 307

Fat 28g

Dietary Fiber 4.1g

Carbohydrates 14.3 g

Protein 3.5g

Skin Cleanser Smoothie

Makes: 5 Servings

Ingredients

1 cup fresh kale (washed and de-stemmed)

1 cup filtered water

1 orange, peeled

1/3 cup pineapple

1/2 cup blueberries

2 tablespoons chia seeds

Directions

Place all of your ingredients into a blender. Blend for 30 seconds.

Pour into tall drinking glasses and add ice. Serve chilled.

Nutrition Facts

Calories 76

Fat 4g

Dietary Fiber 5.2g

Carbohydrates 12g

Protein 3.2g

Conclusion

Low carb smoothies are a great way to get all of the nutrients that your body needs and craves. The best part about them is that they are incredibly easy to digest and taste just as delicious as any other smoothie that you can make. I hope that you come to enjoy these great tasting recipes and that you look forward to showing off these smoothie recipes to all of your friends and family.

When going on a low carb diet and beginning to supplement smoothies into your regular menu, make sure that you start off slow. Start off by supplementing your diet with at least one smoothie a day and make sure to keep eating hearty and healthy meals consisting of fruits, vegetables, whole foods and nuts. Pretty soon you will feel the difference and will find that you have more energy, feel healthier and feel better overall.

Hopefully this book will serve as a guide on your incredible journey and you will be able to come back to it if you ever need inspiration to make your own great tasting low carb smoothie drinks. I wish you the best of luck on your low carb journey.

Made in the USA
Columbia, SC
13 September 2022